FOODFIGHT

ISBN: 978-0-244-96532-7

www.cathypenman.com

FOODFIGHT

Overeating Triggers
and
Strategies to Overcome Them

by

Cathy Penman

Dedicated to

Anyone struggling with weight problems
and compulsive or emotional overeating

Hope it helps

INTRODUCTION

I have spent all my adult life struggling with a weight problem and eating issues. Clearly I'm not the only one – 'obesity' (hateful word) is now regularly referred to as an epidemic; millions of people have the same problems (although it has always seemed like such a personal battle to me).

For years I was so angry about the way slim people view fat people: repeated statements about greed and laziness; criticism of large people taking up too much room on buses and aeroplanes; jokes about people 'eating too many pies'. But worst of all the insinuation that it's a moral weakness not to be able to control your weight, that you are a bad person. Hence the casting of fat people as baddies in films and books; such a cliché, such an insult.

Very recently, I was appalled at a senior person in an anti-obesity organisation using the word 'slob' to describe fat people. So judgemental, so unbelievably unhelpful!

And another phrase I keep coming across is 'fat shaming' – though thankfully often in a context that acknowledges it isn't something which works very well, if the desired effect is to make someone lose weight; they are more likely to go and eat more as a result of being mocked and criticised.

The point is – by definition, the people who don't have a weight problem ARE able to control their eating. But lots of other people clearly can't. When someone makes a comment like, 'just eat less', I want to say to them – yes, maybe that's easy for you, but what if someone has tried, over and over again, but isn't succeeding with the objective of eating less? What do you do then? Basically, the solution isn't that simple.

Luckily, at last, I get the impression that the medical and scientific establishment, and to a certain extent society, has caught up, and is looking at the problem in other ways.

Please – it's NOT about greed and laziness; it's NOT about lack of motivation, or not knowing the facts. You can know that you are causing yourself harm, you can know what you need to do to lose weight, but you are unable, despite trying, to succeed.

At last, I hear the beginnings of an understanding that the issue is IN THE MIND. It is BEHAVIOURAL. It is (arguably) a MENTAL ILLNESS. At last, there is acknowledgement and discussion of compulsive eating, emotional overeating and food addiction.

I can see that from the outside, people might think of someone eating too much just as 'over-indulgence'. But it's when you experience it yourself, when (and this is key) you have tried and tried to stop but cannot, that you have to realise it is an addiction, much like an addiction to smoking or alcohol or drugs.

Many years ago I approached an eating disorders association asking why they only supported suffers of anorexia and bulimia, and not those with compulsive eating and weight problems, which I saw as the other side of the same coin. The association acknowledged that overeating was related but said they had insufficient funding to cover that issue.

However, more recently, when I went to an outpatients' eating disorders clinic for therapy, there was a mix of very thin and very large people in the waiting room. It's a funny and sad old world, that one group of people is killing themselves by not eating enough and another by eating too much. But at last (I hope) we've moved a little bit away from the idea that if you've got anorexia (or if you overeat and sick it up) you're ill and need support, but if you're fat (if you overeat but don't sick it up), you're just 'greedy' and morally weak!

As I always used to say – when getting upset about the number of people, for example, in the USA, who are housebound because of being extremely obese (I believe it's around 4 million people), and the horribly voyeuristic TV programmes often associated with such cases... No-one wakes up in the morning and says, 'I think I'll be life-threateningly obese today', 'I think I'll lie here in bed and not be able to get up or go to the loo on my own'. These are extreme consequences of people not having been able to control their own behaviour for all sorts of complex reasons.

A long time ago, I went to some 'Overeaters Anonymous' (OA) meetings and very much associated with the similar problems and feelings other people were describing. But unfortunately I could never relate to the supposed solution, which was basically giving over your will to a 'higher power'. However much they would say that this doesn't have to be 'God', it can be whatever you conceive of as a higher power... well, if you have a scientific and non-religious viewpoint, and you don't believe that there is any higher power to help you, you're not going to find this helpful.

On the other hand, my experience of Cognitive Behavioural Therapy, which I've encountered a few times over the years, seems very much more sensible, and I trust much more as a potential solution. This is an approach that doesn't look for deep-seated emotional reasons behind your eating problems, but just focuses on day to day BEHAVIOUR. What is triggering your behaviours and what can you do to recognise the triggers, and not act on them?

I'm not at all an expert but I guess much of what I've put down in this book relates to Cognitive Behavioural Therapy ideas.

On the subject of having a biological and non-religious approach to things, one other thing always springs to my mind when considering this issue, and again I am so gratified to have seen discussion of it on a couple of documentaries over the past few years, so it's not just me that looks at it in this way!

Consider the evolution of life on this planet, and the gradual development of different species over some 600 million years – from fish to amphibians to dinosaurs to mammals to primates to man. Imagine your own, personal, ancestors going back all that time, generation after generation.

The absolute key driving force behind all life on this planet is survival. To survive, everything has to eat. Food is life.

Every single creature alive on the planet today, and every single creature that ever lived over 600 million years, and every one of your own personal ancestors over all that time, woke up in the morning and thought.. 'what's for breakfast?' ('What am I going to eat today?' 'Where's the best grass?' 'Where did I hide that nut?' 'What's in the fridge?' 'Which restaurant shall I go to?')

It is the most ultimately natural thing for all animals to spend their days, their lives, thinking about what they're going to eat, and going about the place looking for the next food item they can put in their mouths.

This is the backdrop against which your compulsive eating problems are being considered, or judged. It is entirely natural to want to eat. It is entirely natural to want to eat more rather than less. It's the very stuff of survival. It's a positive thing. Animals that didn't fancy eating didn't survive. Animals that ate lots of food, did.

But suddenly, by being so successful as a species, we've created for ourselves an environment, a society, where there is too much food about rather than too little. Suddenly, for the first time, even within human history, we are surrounded by excess of availability. And what happens? Those many of us who carry on responding in the exact same way as 600 million years of other individuals have responded – ie by seeing food and wanting to eat it, lots of it – suddenly we're doing the wrong thing! Now we're 'greedy'. Now we're all struggling against our basic nature and biological needs. Suddenly we've got to change our behaviour to make sure we don't eat too much. Suddenly too much food is more threatening to us than too little.

I think we need to understand that and excuse ourselves a little!

Here's a related observation. You may have heard of the 'marshmallow test'. Rewards given to young children to see whether they can delay gratification. Some would rather eat what they are offered now, even though it means they don't get a greater reward later. They can't wait, they can't resist. But some will resist initial temptation in order to get more in future. Some will go for two marshmallows later rather than one marshmallow now, and these are shown to have 'better life outcomes'.

So the first thing to say is that obviously people are different, we don't all have the same natural responses. But my observation, in relation to why some people have eating problems and some don't, is that maybe this variety of response is an evolutionary advantage WITHIN POPULATIONS. Maybe it's better to have some people who delay and some who don't, maybe that comes from us being opportunists and omnivores and it may mean a better chance for survival of a group or family if their responses and impulses with regard to food aren't the same. (This is the biologist in me coming out again.)

I also wanted to make a comment about motivation (to diet/lose weight). I have always argued that motivation doesn't help. It's not that someone doesn't know what they should do, or doesn't have sufficiently strong reasons to lose weight, I'm sure they have many – it is that they are addicted to food and are unable to stop.

But I've wondered whether to include MOTIVATION as a strategy. For example, if someone offered me 10 million pounds to lose weight, surely that would be sufficient motivation to make me change my ways? I'd like to think so, but would still be afraid I wouldn't be able to do it. I'd like to think that if someone offered me 10 million pounds on one particular occasion, not to eat a donut, surely I would rather have the 10 million pounds, so surely I would be able to resist? This sort of hypothetical conundrum makes you think that of course motivation could make a difference, if something was sufficiently motivating. And yet lots of people get told they must lose weight otherwise they risk death or dreadful health consequences, like blindness and amputations. And not everyone can respond and succeed.

This is such a difficult issue for me – how can there be so many things STILL getting in the way, when the motivation is a life and death issue? It only shows what a difficult and complex topic this overeating business can be.

Another difficult concept related to motivation is 'willpower'. Is this really some sort of character trait or skill that some people have and some people don't have? Is it really, as I've heard said, something like a muscle that can be built up and improved with practice?

It's so difficult to analyse – some people will see lack of willpower as moral weakness again, something linked to greed and laziness. But maybe these strategies I've tried to suggest and explain are ways of building up willpower. Maybe if you don't have willpower naturally, using and developing these strategies will serve as a substitute for it.

Another thing I must say.. Much as I do believe that these behavioural issues are the solution, I have had conversations with people when we consider that perhaps all our food problems are in fact the result of some biochemical imbalance in the body or brain. Is it in fact driven by fluctuations in blood sugar? Is it maybe the fact that sugar and energy aren't getting through properly to the areas that need it, so there is this constant message from the body that you need to eat? Could it be some subtle hormone that's different in different people – that's missing, or in excess, in people with weight problems? It does make me think.. All this ANGST about habits and behaviours and greed and responsibility – one day will they just be able to do a test and say, you're short of such and such hormone or enzyme, here's a tablet that will correct it?

And the next morning you'd wake up and feel different and not want to overeat any more, not be obsessed with food any more. (Hypnosis is something which I'd hoped might have this effect, but the little I've tried hasn't helped me yet.)

Also one must never forget the effect of one's immediate environment. If I'd been alive through the war when there was food rationing and nothing was available, would I have had the same weight problem? If I was living in a poor country, in some village in Mongolia or some lost tribe in the Amazon, or on some secluded island where the same food options just weren't available and life was completely different, I can't believe I would have got to the same weight I have in my current life. So – although I accept it's still my fault and responsibility – we should remind ourselves that we're struggling in a society of plenty, and especially living in a big city, with food options available all around us. Dozens of different takeaway restaurants offering to deliver to our address, fried chicken places on every main road, literally just one or two blocks apart. Supermarkets everywhere, small shops selling chocolate all over the place, restaurants, pubs, cafés – a city full of options, of food choices, of temptation. Us large people are the products (I won't say victims) of the environment around us, maybe of the successful advertising of corporations seeking to make profit from our weakness. I read yesterday that just one of the many pizza delivery chains in the UK sells a pizza to someone EVERY THREE SECONDS. A small frozen pizza in a box from a supermarket is 1000 calories, so a huge deep meat and fat-laden one from a delivery place is probably 2000 calories in one go. No wonder people struggle, no wonder people despair.

But keep a sense of perspective. Compulsive eating is such a 'first world problem' – struggling not to eat too much in a world of plenty. Think of people elsewhere who don't have enough to eat – I know this can be a cliché, a mother reminding her child of starving children when they eat too much. But nevertheless – remember that you have this particular problem because you are in this particular environment. You might have a much worse problem, that you wouldn't ever be able to fix however hard you tried. (Not being able to find enough food to stay alive.)

This book

So – I first conceived this book after a few months of compulsive eating therapy where there was a focus on overeating triggers, which was quite revelatory. Being asked to write down what you were thinking when you ate something, and what was the trigger that made you eat at that point. (It might just have been waking up, or the time of day, but was often more varied and complex.)

But, as with my experience of the 'higher power' solution at OA, I thought the therapy was less helpful on finding solutions and ways to counter, or overcome, the triggers which had been identified. That's why I've poured all my thinking and ideas into this book, to try to help with that issue. Which at the end of the day, in my opinion, is where the answer to all overeating and weight issues lies (and hence the solution to the worldwide obesity crisis!)

We need to learn how to counteract and overcome the various overeating triggers.

Now I had always intended a book which cross-referenced the triggers with the strategies or solutions, that is, suggested which solution might best apply to which trigger.

However after attempting to do this, with the use of several large tables/schedules, I have changed my mind. It just works out too complicated – there are too many permutations and they are all debatable. So – and I hope you will understand and accept this as a sensible and pragmatic approach – I've decided to drop the idea of detailed cross-referencing, which in any case could be seen as rather patronising and insulting to the reader.

I am sure the reader will recognise the triggers I have described; no doubt many will be familiar. And I'm sure the reader will see the connections with possible strategies to counter them. So I think it's more sensible to leave the reader to consider which triggers apply most to them, and which of the strategies and solutions might best help them in their own struggle.

Let me just make a few suggestions as examples, to give you an idea:

For the DISTRESS trigger, use:
SELF-NURTURING or
ALTERNATIVE COMFORT

For the BOREDOM trigger, use:
MINDFULNESS/MEDITATION or
EXERCISE

For the SEEING FOOD trigger, use:
GOLLUM or
POSTPONEMENT

For the CAN'T STOP trigger, use:
FOOD CONTINUUM or
DRAW A LINE

For the GETTING UP FROM PC trigger, use:
DISTRACTION or
WRITE IT AWAY

For the INDEPENDENCE trigger, use:
COMPROMISE or
SENSE OF RESPONSIBILITY

For FOOD DISAPPOINTMENT, use:
WIN SOME LOSE SOME or
FOOD HISTORY

The strategies I have picked up from receiving therapy and counselling are things like: Nurturing Voice, Distraction and Mindfulness.

The key ones I have sort of formulated myself are Compromise, Postponement and Fussiness – I try to use this trio as my mantra.

Perhaps the strongest, which I find very effective and would advise you to try, is Food Continuum. Also very helpful is Write It Away, and Gollum.

And forgive me if some of the things I've included under strategies are more general, rather than being specific responses to triggers – I've just poured out all my thinking on this topic, in an attempt to help myself and others.

I vs You issue

Many of the comments I have expressed which make up the core of this book, can grammatically either be stated in the first person, 'I', or in the second, 'you'. (Although it is 'you' in the sense of 'one'.)

I have considered going through and making them all consistent, either 'I' or 'you', but sometimes there is a different feel to the expressions, and again I'm sure the reader will understand that in this context the grammar is interchangeable.

To be clear:

'You' means you, the reader.
'I' also means you, the reader!

OVEREATING TRIGGERS

NEED FOR
COMFORT

DISTRESS

DESIRE TO
TRANQUILISE
EMOTIONS

EMOTIONAL CRUTCH

TENSION / STRESS

DEPRESSION

TREATING MYSELF

- I feel so bad
- I can't cope with what's happened
- I know that eating that will make me feel better
- I need a 'salve' to apply to my hurt
- I just want something nice
- I have to have this chocolate bar to 'keep me going'
- There there, poor dear, this will cheer you up
- I need something to take my mind off all this
- I can't bear to think about all my problems
- Oh God, what's the point of anything, let me just bury my head in the pleasure of eating
- I can't deal with my emotions right now, just let me eat
- I am eating to 'fill a hole' (an emotional hole)
- I've got to eat something more before I go into the office, I need it to comfort and bolster me before facing a difficult task

- I can't do a long journey / difficult day like this without eating something
- I've got to meet that awful client this afternoon, I'll have a big meal beforehand to help me cope
- I feel so alone and miserable, food is my best friend, my only friend – don't ask me to desert my best friend
- Food is the only thing I have to look forward to, it cheers me up – it's the highlight of my day
- What's the point of trying to control my eating?
- Why should I give up this comfort? 'Nothing really matters'.
- I'm just going to live for today and take my pleasure where I can
- Things are so bad, I deserve a little pleasure
- It's a 'leisure day' so I'm 'off the leash' – being careful can wait, I'm treating myself today
- A little self-indulgence goes a long way

LONELINESS

GRIEF

BOREDOM

CONVENIENCE

ANGER

- I wish I had someone to talk to about this, never mind I'll make myself a nice meal instead
- I miss him so much, I can't bear to think about it – eating will help
- What on earth am I going to do today? I've had too many days at home alone. Let's go to the supermarket and stock up with nice food.
- This is an intolerable job, I still have another five hours before I can leave, guess I'll go to the shop
- I've walked round this shopping centre so many times, oh here's a new café I can try
- I could NOT be bothered to go and buy fruit! I'm ordering a takeaway.
- I don't do cooking, life's too short to peel potatoes
- How dare she say that to me! I'm so furious I need to eat to calm down.
- Sod it all and damn everyone, I'm just going to treat myself to something nice, so there!
- Don't you dare tell me what to eat!

SEEING FOOD

SEEING FOOD ON TV

SMELLING FOOD

TALKING ABOUT FOOD

THINKING ABOUT FOOD

- Food glorious food! It's natural to want it – grab!
- Wow, that dessert looks nice
- She's eating my favourite burger, where's mine?
- What a fantastic menu, I want everything
- That's so unusual, I must try it, something new
- I must get a wonderful big lamb joint like that
- I can't resist two for one offers on boxes of cakes
- They keep advertising this great new pizza idea
- Cooking programmes on TV so make me want to eat lots and lots of interesting food
- I can smell the neighbours' barbeque again, I'm going out to buy sausages
- Someone's eating chicken and chips on the train, I'll get some for myself on the way home
- Oh, that particular taste reminds me of childhood! Must eat some more of that.
- Everybody's talking about Nigella's new recipe
- Just thought, I haven't had profiteroles for ages
- I've suddenly remembered that lovely pie and mash I saw at the pub yesterday, must go back

CAN'T STOP

INCLUDED IN THE PRICE

BUYING TOO MUCH IN SUPERMARKET

HALF WAY THROUGH A DRINK

- Yes that was very nice, now I want some more
- That wasn't enough
- More more more
- Hasn't hit the spot
- Still don't feel calm
- Still don't feel full
- Haven't had a long enough private eating moment yet
- Well I've eaten half the pack of biscuits, I may as well finish it
- I can't help it, these are so 'moreish'
- I can't watch the rest of this long film without carrying on eating
- There's not many left, I'll just finish off the box
- A few more won't make any difference
- But I've paid bed and breakfast, I can't not have my full English

- It's an 'eat as much as you like' buffet, I haven't had my money's worth yet
- Gosh those people are piling up their plates, why shouldn't I?
- I've bought too much at the supermarket; I can't let all this food go to waste, I'll have to use it up now
- Look at these sell-by dates – I'll have to eat both these things today
- The freezer's empty, I need a few more things
- Oh, I've still got half a cup of coffee left, I need another cake to go with it
- I can't drink this huge drink without some crisps or peanuts to mop it up
- I was only going to have a sandwich, but I've got loads of tea left in this pot, I can't drink it on its own, it needs a donut or at least a biscuit to go with it.

HABIT

ASSOCIATION
EG TV

GETTING UP FROM PC /
BREAK FROM WORK

- Just woke up – where's breakfast?
- 1pm – lunchtime!
- It's Sunday night so I'll have a nice Indian takeaway like I have done for years
- Seaside tomorrow so it's fish and chips
- Sue's bringing the kids so I'll get ice cream
- Whenever I go to our supplier's office, I have to have one of those wonderful bacon sandwiches from that nice place nearby
- I'm sitting down in front of the TV now – I want to eat something
- I'm getting up from my PC after doing a block of work – time to raid the fridge
- I can't sit in a café alone and have a meal without reading a paper or my book
- I'm walking across the station on my way to work in the morning, all sorts of food options around me – I must eat something like I always do
- I'm leaving the office now, what a relief – I need a snack to celebrate regaining my independence

SELF-JUSTIFICATION

INDEPENDENCE

RECKLESSNESS

DENIAL

'I DON'T CARE'

(These are triggers in the sense that they are the thoughts in your head when you make a food decision)

- I'll bloody well eat what I want!
- I've left home now so I'll live my own life and make my own decisions
- How dare the world tell me what I should eat or what size I should be?
- Two fingers up to social norms and public opinion
- I'll just have to face up to any consequences later
- It won't happen to me, I'll risk it
- So I'll just be fat and die early, who cares?
- I don't really mind being large
- Plenty of other people are big
- Nothing wrong with having a bit of a tummy
- I like having larger breasts

SABOTAGE

GAME PLAYING

(Not so much triggers as underlying positions that can influence food decisions and behaviours)

- Part of me gets a secret kick from putting on weight again – see I'm such a difficult case, I won't be cured
- I'm so used to moaning about my weight
- I don't really want to be successful
- I can blame my lack of success on my weight
- 'You're okay, I'm not okay' life position
- Poor me, I can't ever lose weight
- I want to change but I just can't
- I'm not like normal people
- Just forget it and accept you're a failure
- I like wallowing in failure
- I didn't really want a relationship anyway
- I didn't really want children anyway
- I'm scared of sex, so being fat will keep me safe and celibate

FOOD DISAPPOINTMENT

- That was horrible!
- That did not taste nice!
- That was a pathetically small portion!
- That was undercooked
- How dare they serve me something so awful?
- They didn't have my first choice
- Well that was such a horrible meal, I felt tense the whole time about the bad service
- Last time those sandwiches were nice but this time they were so dry and nasty
- I must have something extra / better immediately to compensate for the disappointment!
- Yuk! Didn't hit the spot! Wasn't a positive enough experience! Correction needed.

(It was a revelation to discover that disappointment was such a common overeating trigger for me)

HUNGER

- This is the good one – only eating in response to genuine stomach hunger (and not any of the other / emotional triggers above) is suggested by many as the solution to overeating problems
- Responding to genuine stomach hunger, ie a physiological trigger, is okay, but watch out for overreaction:
- Whee!!! Genuine stomach hunger! Now I can eat whatever I want without guilt, stuff stuff...
- Genuine stomach hunger in the middle of the night – time to get up and raid the fridge
- So – Hunger as a trigger for moderate, controlled eating is natural and good. But hunger – when rarely experienced and in a person with eating issues – can be another trigger, or excuse, for overeating.

- Note some people will say ‘I’m hungry’ or ‘I’m always hungry’, when what they are referring to isn’t genuine stomach hunger, but any of the other eating triggers outlined in this book
- Is this you? Are you really hungry or is it that you just want to eat, for some other, perhaps emotional, reason?
- Some other motivation for eating – a mental motivation – is sometimes referred to as ‘head hunger’
- This is where people with eating problems may differ from those without. Some people genuinely only eat when they feel genuine hunger – if they don’t feel it they just won’t eat. Others may say that they are never truly hungry, but always want to eat.

OTHER POSSIBLE OVEREATING TRIGGERS OR CAUSES

Fear

- I'm scared to go out and meet that person, I'll sit here and eat biscuits instead

Mothering

- My mum makes me such nice meals while I'm living with her, I can't offend her by not eating them
- I have to keep my growing boys fed, it's easier to eat what they eat

Relationship issues

- He refuses to help round the house so why should I try and please him by losing weight?
- He likes me big and I don't want to lose him

Add yours here:

....

....

....

STRATEGIES TO OVERCOME OVEREATING TRIGGERS

STRATEGIES OR SOLUTIONS
OR ANTIDOTES OR TOOLS

OVERCOME OR COUNTER OR
RESIST OR BEAT OR DEAL WITH

COMPROMISE

- *Part of you wants to eat, part of you doesn't – you have to find a compromise between the two positions*
- *You want to eat that huge meal, but you also want to be thinner / healthier*
- *If your desires conflict, you have to choose, you have to compromise*
- *Think, I'd like the immediate pleasure and satisfaction of eating that but it's the sort of food that is making me unwell and healthy, so I'll choose not to have it for my own wellbeing*
- *Say, I'd love to eat that, but I also want to fit into that new dress, so I'll have to pass on that food this time*
- *Think, I've let myself eat a lot recently, so now for a while I won't, I'll compromise with myself*
- *You can't have everything, you're not a spoilt child having a tantrum*

- *Find a way of satisfying both impulses / needs so you're not conflicted*
- *Find a middle ground*
- *At least alternate your responses*
- *Try to diet on alternate days or weeks only*
- *Teach yourself not always to fall on the same side of the decision*
- *Think, sometimes I'll say yes, sometimes I'll say no*
- *Think, I could eat that but I won't on this occasion*
- *You often give in, sometimes you have to not give in*
- *Focus on the positives of the option you're choosing, let the other one go*
- *Allow yourself to eat enough nice things overall that you don't feel deprived and unhappy*
- *Get your needs and desires in balance*
- *Don't let one side of your character keep winning*

POSTPONEMENT

- *Yes, I really want to eat that – but I won't have it now, I'll have it later*
- *You can definitely have that food, just not now*
- *Have it tomorrow, or later in the week, or next time you go to this shop*
- *That's a lovely looking cake, I'll eat it next time I decide to have a cake*
- *I'll put that on the top of the list of things I want to eat next*
- *Make a mental note of what it was you fancied and come back to get it another time*
- *Build up a wishlist of foods you'll have later*
- *I'll make a note of this great restaurant menu, and after I've had a few lower calorie days, I'll come back here and have that lovely looking dish*
- *I'll eat that within tomorrow's calorie allowance, then I can eat it without guilt*
- *I'll eat those things next year, when I'm thinner*

- *It will wait, I'm sure they'll still have it tomorrow*
- *Say, I'll leave that for now, but I'm really looking forward to eating it tomorrow*
- *Say, I'll have that pudding next time, I'll have that new type of sandwich in a few days, I'll have that takeaway once I've lost another six pounds*
- *I don't have to say no to anything, I just have to allow more time to pass before I eat it all*
- *Eat whatever food you want, but on a different time axis*
- *If all the food I'm planning to eat is a big ball of dough, I just have to roll it out thinner with a rolling pin, so it lasts longer*
- *Push the food into the future, spread it out more*
- *The same amount of food but lasting longer, over a longer period*
- *That food will be yours, just delay, postpone, have patience*

FUSSINESS

- *Do I really want that?*
- *How much do I really like those?*
- *I don't really like that kind of sandwich*
- *Last time I had that it wasn't very nice*
- *Those burgers always taste like cardboard*
- *Is that one of my favourite foods / tastes?*
- *Is it a 1 out of 10, or a 10 out of 10 item?*
- *If it's only a 1 or 2 or 3 out of 10, if it doesn't score highly, why not let it go? Why not save those calories for something I like better?*
- *What's the point of eating that when I know I don't like it?*
- *I'll wait till I see something I really fancy*
- *I'll cook myself something nicer than that later*
- *Consider that food item, put it on the shortlist, but wait and see what other alternatives there are*
- *Why not cut out the things you like least and just eat the things you like most?*

FOOD CONTINUUM

- *You see a donut in a shop window and want to eat it*
- *In the back of the shop they've got six more big trays of donuts*
- *That other shop down the road also contains hundreds of donuts*
- *In the bakers where they make these, there are thousands of donuts produced every day*
- *In this country there are hundreds of thousands of donuts all over the place sitting in bakeries, in shops, in cafés, in people's homes*
- *In the world at this moment there are vast quantities of donuts just like this one*
- *You can't possibly eat all those*
- *This donut is just part of a vast food continuum*
- *You are just one person, surrounded by a vast food continuum*
- *There are millions of donuts you will never eat*

- *Visualise yourself in a room packed full of donuts*
- *Visualise yourself pushing your way through a sea of donuts*
- *There is a vast quantity of food in the world, being consumed by billions of people*
- *Food spreads out around you, the world is full of food, in every shop and restaurant and café everywhere – you'll never eat it all*
- *You're not going to eat the third donut from the right in that café in that other city*
- *You're never going to eat that donut currently on that production line in that other country*
- *So why do you have to eat this particular donut in front of you, just because you've seen it?*
- *You'll never eat all that other food out there in the world, you don't have to eat all the food you see*
- *Push the donut back into the rest of the food continuum and ignore it*

MOVE THE LINE

- *Visualise a table with a huge food buffet laid out, just for you*
- *You couldn't possibly eat it all*
- *Take all the food you intend to eat now and put it in one place*
- *So there is an invisible 'line' between the food you have decided to eat and the food that's still there but you can't eat, it's too much even for you*
- *There is always going to be more food available that even you can't eat*
- *Why draw the line – between what you will and won't eat – THERE, and not THERE?*
- *Move that arbitrary line so it's closer to you – put some of the food you were going to eat into the section you weren't going to eat*
- *The position of that line represents your problem – experiment with shifting the line*
- *You can choose where to draw it*

FOOD HISTORY

- *Picture all the food you ate yesterday set out on a table*
- *Add the food from the day before*
- *Now think of all the food you ate last month, last year – food you have already enjoyed*
- *Years and years of food you have previously eaten, set out on a long, long table*
- *All that food has been put into your body*
- *All that food has passed through your body*
- *You are like a giant worm, chomping your way through food day after day – in one end, out the other*
- *You can control the flow of it, slow it down*
- *Do you really have to eat that pasty now?*
- *Think of all the other pasties you've ever eaten lined up behind you*
- *It's not like you've never eaten a pasty before*
- *Why one more?*

GOLLUM

- *There are two sides to your character, the sensible side which has a noble purpose, and the side which is all about self-gratification and desire*
- *This is like Smeagol / Gollum in The Lord of the Rings. Imagine the disgusting, ugly, selfish Gollum crawling on the floor in front of you, holding up a plate full of fried chicken and chips.*
- *He is tempting and taunting you – 'Eat this, eat this, you know you want to; mmm greasy, fatty'*
- *He represents your baser urges and desires – don't let him influence you, don't let him distract you from your higher purpose (losing weight / being healthy / staying alive)*
- *Look down at Gollum contemptuously and say, dismissively, 'No thank you!'*
- *'You can squirm and beg as much as you want, I don't want that fried chicken, and that's final!'*
- *Go away – I'm not listening – Talk to the hand!*

CONSCIOUS VS SUBCONSCIOUS

- *Gollum can be seen as your subconscious. Don't let the unconscious urge that he represents influence you all the time / so much.*
- *Say, I must not let my subconscious urges and habits derail my conscious decisions*
- *'Reason commands, appetite obeys'. Don't allow your appetite to completely overrule your reason.*
- *Don't allow your mind to be undisciplined*
- *Recognise when it's a subconscious urge making you want to overeat – and reject it*
- *Who should make decisions about your life – your conscious or your subconscious?*
- *Take back control*
- *Don't consolidate your food addiction by repeatedly giving in to subconscious urges and associations*
- *The conscious needs to fight back*
- *Your 'heart' may long for self-indulgence, but your 'head' knows better*

SELF-NURTURING

NURTURING VOICE

- *There, there, you poor thing*
- *What a dreadful day you've had*
- *Anyone would be feeling tense after that!*
- *Don't upset yourself*
- *Leave that food for now, you don't need it. Just have a little cry, have a little sit and a think, don't bury your head in the comfort of food.*
- *I'm sure you can manage to get through this without having to eat*
- *Imagine saying these things to someone else, someone who had asked you for help. Imagine yourself coaching and helping them, then imagine coaching yourself*
- *Try to find someone else to help you if you can, but if that's not possible, take on that role yourself*
- *Imagine you are a caring adult talking to a troubled child*

- *This is the 'adult' me, or the 'nurturing parent' me, talking to the distressed 'child' me, giving that child comfort and reassurance, using the strong side of my own character to help and support the weaker, more needy side*
- *Nurture yourself, be your own perfect nurturing parent*
- *Take my hand and we'll walk across this station together without eating*
- *I'll help you get through this, I'll support you*
- *Look for comfort within yourself, not without*
- *You can help yourself better than anything in the outside world can help you*
- *You don't need the food, you can live through this without it*
- *Forget about that food, it's not doing you any good really, is it?*

- *Food doesn't care about you, or about the harm and consequences it can cause. You can care about you.*
- *Think about self-esteem – is it something you are lacking, and how can you build it up?*
- *Don't let self-esteem depend on looks or size or weight, find a core of self-esteem in yourself and focus on it*
- *Help yourself to nurture your self-esteem*
- *Be strong, have confidence in yourself*
- *Don't worry, be happy*
- *'This too will pass'*

(Comment: Ten or twenty years ago in the UK I believe there was more of a 'movement' of large women trying to look at themselves positively. There were magazines for large women talking about loving your size, accepting yourself as you are, being fat and fit. There were nightclubs specifically for big women, 'celebrating' their size, being positive about having curves. All this came from the US where there is perhaps still a stance from some groups that being fat isn't so bad. This is where the concept of being 'BBW' came from. 'Big Beautiful Women'. But somehow now this positive voice seems to have been subsumed by all the negative messages about obesity and healthy eating, so you now very seldom see any sort of opinion that perhaps you can just BE FAT and accept yourself, and not try to change. Writing about self-nurturing has reminded me about all this, and made me realise that I suppose I have never accepted the 'fat is okay' message, and come down on the side of that being big is unhealthy and that one does need to change. It's made me think again though, about the overall concept. Can't we be free to just abandon all this angst and be large if we want to? Does everyone have to be thin? Can't there be more of a variety of acceptable size in society?)

IDENTIFY THE FEELING

SIT WITH THE FEELING

- *Give a name to the emotion you're feeling*
- *Is it an emotion or a thought?*
- *Are you sure that's it? Are there other emotions also?*
- *Are there underlying emotions? – What's really going on?*
- *What's getting in the way of you reacting or behaving in a more sensible and rational fashion?*
- *Thinking about what you're feeling might calm you down enough to make a different food decision*
- *Just 'sit with' whatever it is you are feeling – think about it, look at it, acknowledge it (rather than use food to dull it or avoid it)*
- *Having a feeling doesn't have to lead to a particular action*
- *Unhook your usual response from that feeling*

IS THAT REALLY HELPING YOU NOW?

- *Is it really helping you at this point to respond to that emotion by stuffing yourself?*
- *Is it really helping you to get so upset over and influenced by what someone else looks like?*
- *Is buying that huge bar of chocolate really going to help you right now?*
- *That lovely takeaway may seem like a good idea, but is it really helping you in the long run?*
- *Really?? Step back and think again.*
- *Maybe not a good idea?*

DISTRACTION

- *Whoops, a food-lust has leapt into your mind – immediately think of something else*
- *Make an effort to push it out of your mind*
- *Quickly occupy your mind with other thoughts*
- *Do something different*
- *Get up and go to the loo*
- *Go for a walk and count steps*
- *Phone a friend for a chat*
- *Listen to music*
- *Pick up a good book*
- *Get absorbed in a crossword*
- *Play an electronic game*
- *Go do that chore you meant to do yesterday*
- *Go shopping*
- *Paint your nails*
- *Wash your hair*
- *Recite a poem, or say a prayer*
- *Do a times table*

- *Count the number of squares on the carpet*
- *Count backwards from a thousand*
- *Go through the alphabet and think of a country beginning with each letter*
- *Think through what you did yesterday*
- *How many people's names can you remember from your school days?*
- *Quick, think about your last holiday – how many different places / experiences can you remember?*
- *Imagine what clothes you'll buy if you get thin*

Food urges are known to abate. Distract yourself for a few minutes, and it may go away. 'Surf the urge'

Cross check an eating urge against ASSOCIATION *– is it just a pathway in your brain linking things together? Consciously break the link.*

In more general terms:

- *Find some new project to throw your energies into so you're not always dwelling on food issues*
- *Focus on a career plan or start a business*
- *Do charity work – turn your attention outward, towards helping other people rather than just being over-involved with yourself*
- *Find someone to fall in love with (at least spend some time trying) – the distraction of a new relationship might help*
- *Always keep busy*
- *Fill your life with other stuff you find rewarding so you're not so preoccupied with the daily battle with food*

WRITE IT AWAY

- *At the actual moment of feeling the eating urge, grab a pen and paper and start writing about the situation and your feelings – the act of writing can diffuse and dispel the urge. Keep writing until it's gone, until your mood / mindset has changed.*

Write in a flow of consciousness; no-one will ever see what you write, you won't even keep or re-read it. Just write things like this, call on the strategies you find most effective from this book:

"Oh dear, I'm having another food urge, I really really want to eat another one of those cakes now – so I need to distract myself and recognise that it's just a thought in my head that I don't have to act on – I've done this before and I know that if I just focus on writing for five or ten minutes it can seem like magic, the eating urge will just go away, IT WILL PASS"

"Think about all the cakes you've eaten in the past – there are thousands of cakes like that in the world right now, you don't have to eat that particular one – think of something else, let it go, maybe this is some slight chemical imbalance in your blood or brain that is making you want it, but in a moment you won't want it any more, your feelings will change and this decision will be history – you can't always eat cake after cake just because you've seen it or the fancy takes you – be more responsible about what you put into yourself – overeating is causing you misery, so you need to work to leave it behind…"

"Think about what happened at work today, or the plot of that film you saw, or what you want for Christmas, distract your mind with other thoughts... see, the urge has lessened now, you're not that bothered any more.."

ALTERNATIVE COMFORT

Overlaps with some suggestions under DISTRACTION eg

- *Phone a friend for a chat*
- *Listen to music*
- *Go shopping – retail therapy!*

Try also

- *Hug a cuddly toy*
- *Stroke a pet*
- *Have a nice hot bath with lots of bubbles*
- *Sit down and write a list of ten wonderful moments you remember in your life*
- *Sit down and write a list of all the friends you have had in your life*
- *Think about a good relationship you currently have, or have had – dwell on the details, think of nice moments*

- *DON'T turn to smoking or drinking*
- *DON'T turn to drugs – this will become a bigger problem!*
- *Consider turning to sex instead of food, if it's available and it works for you – but watch out for sex addiction*
- *Sex (or lack of it) might actually be a trigger for overeating rather than a solution*

- *Think of the sense of achievement you will get from having lost weight and overcome your eating problems – think of the rewards and comfort that will bring you*

MINDFULNESS / MEDITATION

- *When the eating urge hits – recognise it as just a thought or a feeling*
- *Do 'thought watching' meditation – you don't have to act on the thought, just observe it from the outside*
- *Project yourself outside of the current situation*
- *Immediately imagine yourself at a point in the future AFTER YOU HAVE AVOIDED THE URGE / TRIGGER AND DECIDED NOT TO EAT*
- *Look at the clock and add two hours*
- *Where are you sitting, what does the room look like, the sofa feel like?*
- *Look back on the decision point – imagine yourself thinking of it in the past*
- *Think, I experienced a food urge/ trigger but I just put it out of my mind quickly and didn't act on it*
- *Focus on yourself thinking, I'm so glad I didn't order that pizza, because now the urge is gone*

THOUGHT WATCHING

- *Step outside your mind and look at your thoughts from the outside*
- *Say, there's a thought that says, I want to eat something*
- *Just look at it, acknowledge it as a thought – you don't have to act on it*
- *A thought doesn't have to lead to an action*
- *It's just electric impulses in your brain*
- *Wait, observe*
- *Say, oh look, I'm having an eating urge again*
- *There's another eating urge, maybe it'll go away in a minute*
- *Just because I've smelt a nice food smell doesn't mean I have to have that food now*
- *Say, that's a nice smell, I must eat that sometime soon*

MINDFUL EATING

- *Analyse how often you eat in front of the TV or reading a book or paper or looking at your phone (in my case it was 100% of the time, and I truly hadn't realised)*
- *This makes you eat 'on automatic', and hence not notice what you are eating, and not be satisfied, so eat more*
- *Try, and practise frequently, eating without the TV or book or tablet – ie mindful eating*
- *It can be very difficult in the first few moments, because of the strong association and habit, but this passes and after a while the eating becomes a different experience*
- *Be aware of eating 'in the now'*
- *Let yourself enjoy the taste and texture of the food, let yourself get enjoyment from it*
- *Focus on the food, not something else*

- *Make eating the main thing you're doing, not just an extra thing*
- *Be aware of the half way point, think, I've still got half of this plateful to go*
- *I still haven't finished it, there's still more for me to enjoy*
- *Deliberately try different foods with different textures as a mindful eating exercise – eg raisins, rice pudding, lychees, biltong, sorbet, peas, crackers – and eat them very slowly*
- *Experiment with having a different experience of eating than usual*

BAT IT AWAY

- *See the eating urge coming towards you like a ball flying through the air*
- *Visualise yourself holding a baseball bat – it is broad and you are expert, you do not miss*
- *With all your might you swipe at the ball and hit it hard*
- *There it goes, sailing away from you, way out of sight*
- *So much for the eating urge – it's gone, you've batted it far away from you*
- *Here comes the next one, whack, that's that sorted*
- *Any more coming this way? You'll be ready for them*
- *The more you've practised batting them away, the easier it will be*

JUMP OVER

- *Here comes the eating urge, you've spotted it*
- *Don't let it derail you, knock you over*
- *It's like an animal running fast towards you, or an object zooming towards you on a conveyor belt*
- *See it, prepare for it*
- *Jump over the eating urge, leave it behind*
- *Whiz, there it is zooming away behind you*
- *You've avoided it, you've jumped over it and it's gone*
- *See, it's passed you by without having an effect*
- *Now turn around and get ready to jump over the next one*
- *The food urges are going to keep coming but you're going to get so used to jumping over them, they won't be a problem at all*
- *Jump over the space between meals, jump from one meal to the next*

DRAW A LINE UNDER

- *You have finished eating for now*
- *Draw a line under that meal*
- *Visualise drawing a thick line with a marker pen*
- *That's that meal over, now do something else until the next*
- *You are now in a non-eating vs an eating period*
- *You are not in 'eating mode' until the next planned meal*
- *Visualise flicking a switch into a different position – you've switched yourself to non-eating mode now*
- *I'm about to eat my lunch – this is me eating my lunch – now I have finished my lunch*
- *However preoccupied with food you think you are, no-one eats all the time – there are lots of times when you are not eating. Think about the food-free periods of each day – you CAN not eat.*
- *Make the barriers clearer, don't let food encroach into the non-food parts of the day*

SEE ALSO 'ON / OFF SWITCH'

ON / OFF SWITCH

- *Some people have a clearer on / off switch with regard to eating. If you have overeating problems, you don't have – you need to reinforce your on / off switch.*
- *Picture a giant on / off switch – move it to 'off'*
- *It's on when it needs to be, to keep you alive – then turn it off, forget about food*
- *You are no longer in eating mode, you are in 'doing other things in your life' mode*
- *You cannot keep eating more and more and more and more in one session. Flick a switch, close a door, build a dam to stop the flow of food.*

SEE ALSO 'DRAW A LINE UNDER'

ADJUST THE DIALS

- *Imagine a series of round dials in front of you, like on some old radio or piece of equipment*
- *Turn down the 'I need comfort' dial to a lower setting*
- *Turn down the 'I've just got to eat what I want now' dial to a lower setting*
- *Turn down the 'I give up, I'll never conquer this' dial to a lower setting*
- *Turn up the 'taking personal responsibility' dial to a higher setting*
- *Turn up the 'time to change' and 'self-nurturing' dials to a much higher setting*
- *Get used to retuning your triggers and responses*
- *Alternatively whenever you experience a trigger, imagine pushing a 'mute' button – you can't hear it now, you've silenced it.*
- *Or – imagine pressing a 'reset' button, clear your mind of previous influence*

DRAGON IN CAVE

- *The food urge is like a dragon in a cave, or a pen*
- *He's often asleep and not bothering you, but sometimes he wakes up and demands massive amounts of food*
- *He is your eating urge, all your eating triggers, animated and personified*
- *Use COMPROMISE to throw him some bits of food to keep him happy*
- *Keep him locked up so he can't get to you*
- *Shout at him like a naughty dog – oh, be quiet and go to sleep*
- *Visualise shooting a tranquiliser dart into him*
- *Can he ever be killed completely, by a knight with a sword? Or will you have to live with him for ever, in which case you need to manage him, keep him happy, keep him asleep as much as possible.*

WIN SOME, LOSE SOME

- *I’m so disappointed by that food, but I don’t have to react to that disappointment by eating more, I can just make a note not to choose the same thing again*
- *Well, I really didn’t like that sandwich, but do I really have to go and immediately eat something else to make up for it?*
- *Yuk! That was horrible and I’m furious, but I need to calm down about it*
- *Everything I eat can’t be perfect*
- *I can’t react like a spoilt child*
- *If I watched a film I thought was poor, I wouldn’t immediately go and see a second one I thought might be better, to make up for it*
- *Demanding consolation for a minor bad experience is ridiculous*
- *Wait till next time, write it off*
- *You win some, you lose some*

TAKE RESPONSIBILITY

SENSE OF RESPONSIBILITY

COMMON SENSE

PERSPECTIVE

MATURITY

- *Just because you want something doesn't mean you should have it*
- *You are not obliged to give in to every urge – you can choose how you act*
- *Take responsibility for what you put into your own body / your own choices / your own wellbeing*
- *At the end of the day no-one can help you but yourself*
- *Consider whether the 'adult' side of your character has indulged or spoilt the 'child' side too much. It needs to provide support and nurturing but not too much indulgence. The 'child' side also needs to recognise the need for maturity and not demand comfort and gratification all the time.*
- *Re 'half a cup of coffee left' trigger – Just grow up, don't be so silly, drink the rest of the cup on its own!*

AUTHORITATIVE VOICE

(Although beware, many would say the authoritative voice results in 'beating yourself up', and the nurturing voice is more effective.)

- *Don't be such a child! Control yourself!*
- *Do not even think about eating more of that now, are you mad?*
- *I think you know better than that, show some strength and maturity!*
- *Use your / develop some willpower!*
- *Exert some impulse control!*
- *Don't keep pushing things out of your mind – face the issues!*
- *'You can think about it, but don't do it!'*
- *Stop making excuses! Only when you've recognised that you're always making excuses for your behaviour can you move forward*
  (A sentiment often expressed on US 'bootcamp' type programmes)

CONSEQUENCES

- *If you keep eating like this you will get ill*
- *Do you want to have a heart attack?*
- *Do you want your life to be ruined by a stroke?*
- *'Change your life before it changes you'*
- *Where do you want to be in 5 years time?*
- *Poor health may affect your mobility – do you want to not be able to walk?*
- *Do you want to be housebound, or free to enjoy the world?*
- *If you have or get diabetes, it may affect your eyesight – do you want to go blind for the sake of eating too many cakes?*
- *Which part of BLIND do you not understand?*
- *Diabetes complications can happen quickly – do you want your feet amputated next year?*
- *You have to consider the consequences of your choices, of your lifestyle*

I'M FULL UP

- *I'm going to really try and stop eating when I've reached my 'full up' point – it's easier to recognise that than to recognise genuine hunger*
- *Listen to your body, don't ignore the full up signal, it's the solution to your problems*
- *Be brave enough to STOP when you get the first full up signal – leave the rest on your plate, put it back in the fridge*
- *Combine with POSTPONEMENT – I'm full now so I'll leave the rest till later / tomorrow*
- *Combine with DRAW A LINE UNDER – as soon as I feel full, I'll draw a firm line, I'll use the full up signal as my switch to non-eating mode*
- *On occasions when you feel full, use MINDFULNESS to focus and dwell on that feeling – to draw it to your mind's attention, make sure you're familiar with it*

SUBSTITUTION

- *I'm so, so desperate to eat – but maybe I can try just having some of those carrot sticks or an apple instead of going out to buy chocolate*
- *I really haven't had enough, I want another plateful of food just like that one – but let's try just drinking two glasses of water instead for now*
- *It's so cold and miserable and a pizza would be fantastic – but maybe I'll start with a couple of these cup-a-soups first and see if that does the trick*
- *Good thing I've got all those low calorie ready meals in the freezer, maybe one of the Indian or Chinese ones will do tonight, instead of ordering another takeaway*

SEE ALSO 'DISTRACTION' AND 'ALTERNATIVE COMFORT'

EXERCISE

- *When any trigger stimulates a desire for food, try substituting exercise for eating as the reaction*
- *Eg for the 'Getting up from the PC' trigger, instead of eating something, try doing 10 or 20 step ups on an exercise step or the first step of your staircase*
- *When food crosses your mind, go for a walk round the block*
- *If you see something you want in a shop or café, run up some stairs instead (remind yourself of the consequences of eating too much and being unfit)*
- *If you're bored, try an exercise video rather than cooking a meal; look into yoga*
- *If you're angry, run on the spot until you're tired*
- *Use with POSTPONEMENT – I'll try exercise first, the eating urge might go away*
- *Dance, dance, dance – it will cheer you up*

BEHAVIOUR EXPERIMENT

- *Well, normally in this situation I would eat, but just this once I'll try not eating and see what happens*
- *Do I feel worse? Does the food urge go away?*
- *Am I really unable to cope unless I eat?*
- *Do I feel how I expected to feel?*
- *Maybe I'll actually feel better if I don't eat*
- *Maybe by reacting differently I will gradually gain strength*
- *I'll try EXERCISE as a reaction to a food urge for a week, see how it goes*
- *I'll try calling a friend to talk if I feel bad, instead of turning to food, and see if anything changes*
- *Experiment with the idea of abstinence, see how it feels*
- *My behaviour has to change or I will never change*

QUALITY VS QUANTITY

- *Maximise enjoyment of food by going for food of high quality*
- *Learn to really appreciate good food tastes*
- *When eating something really good, use MINDFULNESS to concentrate on it and make the pleasure of eating it last*
- *Work on your cooking skills or try fine dining*
- *Instead of eating burgers and chips again, buy some posh ingredients from a nice shop and cook a spectacular recipe*
- *Stop spending so much on pizza and go to a better restaurant occasionally instead*
- *Hold back on calories during the week so you can really enjoy a nice meal when you go away for the weekend*
- *Use 'quality not quantity' as a matra*

SEE ALSO 'FUSSINESS'

RESILIENCE

- *Practice not giving up*
- *If things don't go well one day, don't feel this means you will never overcome your problems*
- *Just put it aside and try again the next day*
- *If GOLLUM wins one day, try and beat him the next – try and increase the proportion of days where Smeagol wins instead of Gollum*
- *Don't get caught up with failure*
- *Don't get dragged down by self-critical thoughts*
- *Be resilient*
- *Keep trying*
- *Stay positive*
- *Other people succeed, so can you*
- *Be inspired by other people's success stories*

PLANNING

- *Be aware of potential triggers and have a plan in advance – think through what strategies you can use when triggers arise*
- *If you know you always have a strong urge to eat when getting up from the PC or sitting down to the TV, use SUBSTITUTION – have some low calorie things ready, as part of a daily allowance, so that there is something sensible available to meet that urge – eg a banana, some slices of apple, a stick of celery, a bowl of nuts. Or use DISTRACTION – have a book ready, or a phone number you can call for a chat as soon as you finish your work.*
- *If you know when you see a certain takeaway or street food market, that you will be tempted, avoid those places! Use MINDFULNESS to imagine yourself walking past them, choosing a different route.*

- *If you know you are likely to buy too much from a supermarket, go with a very clear advance plan to only buy, for example, food for one or two nights. Use FOOD CONTINUUM and POSTPONEMENT to counter all the other things you see and want – have them next time.*
- *If someone asks you to go for cake and coffee, and you really don't want to eat more cake, use GOLLUM, secretly imagine a horrible creature tempting you, and say no to its influence*
- *If you get invited to a meal out, plan for that food to be within a calorie allowance – use COMPROMISE, have a couple of sensible days beforehand so that you can then have the nice meal you want in company, and go back to being careful afterwards*

- *Plan particularly for emotional reaction. If you have to face something difficult, SIT WITH YOUR FEELINGS before eating afterwards. If you know you are meeting a difficult person, use SELF-NURTURING to help yourself through it (instead of using food as a crutch).*
- *If you know you are facing three particularly boring days ahead, spend some time in advance planning how to keep your mind busy, and how to avoid turning to food. Use EXERCISE to break up the days, use SENSE OF RESPONSIBILITY to keep perspective and stay in control. Prepare yourself to use THOUGHT WATCHING, so that when food thoughts and urges occur, you can recognise them as just thoughts which you knew were coming. Then you can BAT THEM AWAY.*
- *On a busy and stressful day, use DRAGON IN CAVE – keep him happy with sensible snacks*

*THIS IS **NOT** A STRATEGY!*
*THIS IS HOW YOU SHOULD **NOT** REACT TO OVEREATING TRIGGERS!*

SELF-CRITICISM BEATING YOURSELF UP CALLING YOURSELF NAMES

- *These are the sorts of thoughts that people with overeating problems will be familiar with and that create the vicious circle that makes it difficult to stop / change*
- *These thoughts can be triggers in themselves*
- *Push these thoughts aside, do not think them! They are NOT HELPFUL, they don't bring about change.*
- *Think nurturing thoughts and work on changing habits and responses to specific overeating stimuli*
- *WORK ON CHANGING BEHAVIOUR*

- *I am so fat*
- *I am so greedy*
- *I am such a slob*
- *I am so weak and useless*
- *I am so pathetic*
- *I'm such a failure*
- *I am such an embarrassment*
- *I am disgusting*
- *I am so unattractive / ugly*
- *I hate my body*
- *My legs are so fat*
- *My bum is so big*
- *My face is so flabby*
- *I can't bear to look in a mirror*
- *I can't bear to look at photos of myself*
- *I feel so bad about myself*
- *No-one will want me*
- *No-one will love me*

- *No wonder he / she doesn't want me*
- *I'm a disappointment to my parents*
- *I'm such a huge size*
- *I'm so much bigger than my friends*
- *I look dreadful in these clothes*
- *Everyone will laugh at me*
- *I should lock myself away*
- *No wonder I haven't got a partner*
- *No wonder I can't find a job*
- *I will never look as good as her / him*
- *I will never be thin*
- *There is no way out*
- *I know I'll do the same tomorrow*
- *I'm stuck in a vicious circle*
- *I'm a food addict*
- *I will never change*
- *My life is a mess*
- *I hate myself*

Author's Honesty Note

Have I completely overcome my eating problems? No.

Have the ideas I have put down in this book helped me make good progress? Yes.

I am convinced that recognising the various triggers that are making you turn to food and finding ways to deal with them, is the key.

#0146 - 060818 - C0 - 210/148/8 - PB - DID2268647